WHERE THE
clouds
MEET THE
stars

SABINA LAURA

ABOVE THE
clouds
MEET THE
stars

SABINA LAURA

Copyright © Sabina Laura
All rights reserved.

No portion of this book may be used or reproduced without written permission from the author except for the use of brief quotation in book reviews or scholarly journals.

Edited by Shelby Leigh
Interior illustrations © Creative Market

ISBN: 9798321568668

head in the clouds ... 2

castles in the sky ... 28

feet on the ground ... 54

written in the stars ... 80

maybe i'm being reckless.
maybe i'm letting my heart
guide me down the wrong path,
but i cannot help following it
when i know it's leading me to you.
because even if you never
reach out to catch me,
even if you never so much as
look in my direction,
there is nothing better
than seeing you at the other end
of the fall.

you wonder why i keep chasing these dreams,
but there is nothing to lose when your hands are
too full of hope to ever be empty.

maybe one of these daydreams will be close
enough to hold in your palms, or maybe it'll
disappear into a sky that has to end somewhere.

but you never know where just *believing* might
take you. after all, beautiful stories never begin
with a heart that's ready to give up.

i don't know where
all this waiting for you will end up,
but when i imagine life
with you by my side,
the view is incredible.

maybe i'm looking
through rose-tinted glasses
or maybe we really could feel like
a sunrise that illuminates the horizon.

maybe i'm getting
caught up in the idea of us,
or maybe you really will be
the miracle i've been waiting for.

i guess we'll never know until we try.

all i *do* know is that my dreams
show me a future worth fighting for.

i'm still holding out hope
for our love story,
waiting for fate
to take a chance on us,
wondering when it'll be our turn
in the spotlight.

because i don't want us to
only ever be an *almost*.
i don't want us to
give up on this before
it's even begun.

we deserve to know
what this could become.

i am ready to jump if you are,
so take my hand and close your eyes.

because it feels like everything in my life
has been leading up to this moment,
like loving you could just be
the most incredible thing
i have ever done.

that's why i am no longer afraid
of how i might land.

I HAVE BEEN WAITING A LIFETIME
TO FALL FOR YOU.

loving you
has turned my world
upside down
in the best way,
and it feels like
i'm exactly where
i'm meant to be.

— *head over heels*

we could spend so long
waiting for the right moment
that we forget to live in it.

we could spend so long
being afraid of the unknown
that we miss its magical opportunities.

or we could lose ourselves in the falling
and worry about the landing later.

we could trust that if it's meant to be,
it will work out perfectly.

I LIVE IN BLACK AND WHITE BUT MY DREAMS ARE STILL MADE OF COLOUR.

*don't worry if you feel like
you've lost yourself somewhere along the way.*

*i have memorised you better than myself
and i will always know where to find you.*

i fall asleep knowing
i'll be chasing dreams
all through the night,
and i wake up ready to see
which ones will find me
with eyes wide open.

because there is no horizon
that doesn't look like hope
when you see all that light
rising above it,
and each new day brings
the chance to start again.

i want to learn every shade of you,
so don't be afraid to show me
all the colours that make you *you*.

because i already know for certain
that i will love your dark
just as much as your light.

you make
my monochrome world
more vibrant than i could ever imagine,
and i am already seeing in colours
i never knew existed.

my dreams
will always be
as big as the sky,
but sometimes that sky
is more setting sun
than anything else.

but that's okay. after all,
there is always a new dawn.
there is always a new dream.

*i just hope
we never let go of each other,
no matter how many winters
may come our way.*

i would rather be
by your side
in the pouring rain
than be in the sunshine
with anyone else.

it doesn't need to be perfect.
it just needs to be you.

THERE IS

SO MUCH DARKNESS

IN BETWEEN MY

FULL-MOON DREAMS,

BUT THIS HOPE

WILL BE ENOUGH

TO LIGHT

THE ENTIRE SKY.

*i've always been lost
in dreams of being found,
but i'm just hoping you'll be the one
to know me by heart.*

you were the plot twist
i never saw coming,
but sometimes love shows up
when you least expect it
and turns out to be everything
you never knew you needed.

you have changed my story for the better
and i'm already hoping you'll stay
until the very last page.

i'm tumbling
towards the earth
because the clouds promised
they would catch me
if you didn't.

but now that i've let go,
it feels like there's nothing to fear.

i'm falling for you,
but it feels more like flying.

I'M LOST

IN A DAYDREAM,

FLOATING AMONGST

HOPE-COLOURED CLOUDS.

THEY TELL ME

TO PUT MY FEET

BACK ON THE GROUND,

BUT THIS VIEW

IS TOO BEAUTIFUL

TO MISS.

time stands still
when i'm with you.

the earth keeps spinning,
but nothing around us matters.

because it's just you and me
in our own little world, and i swear—
i could stay here forever.

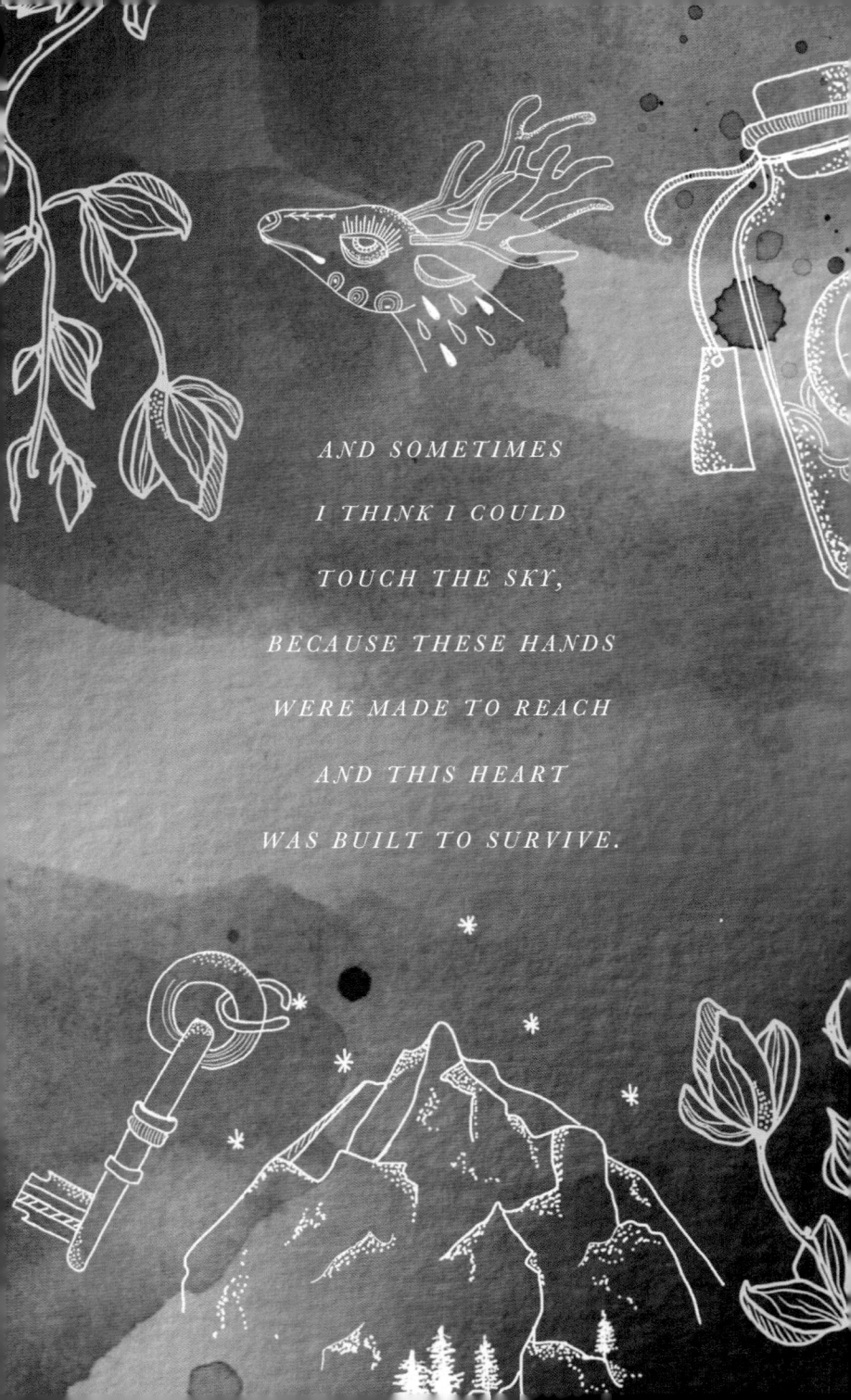

*AND SOMETIMES
I THINK I COULD
TOUCH THE SKY,
BECAUSE THESE HANDS
WERE MADE TO REACH
AND THIS HEART
WAS BUILT TO SURVIVE.*

CASTLES

in

the
SKY

the universe didn't believe in us
the way i did, although i still think
we weren't given enough of a chance.

but the truth is,
we were a *right-person-wrong-time* kind of love,
yet that doesn't make it any easier—
knowing that we could've been
so much more than we were.
knowing that in another lifetime,
we might've made it work.

i never know where i am with you.
one minute, i'm over the moon,
and the next, the stars are crashing
down at my feet.

but without you,
i'd be spinning out of orbit,
because you've become
the centre of everything i know.

the truth is,
i'd follow you
to the ends of the earth.

the truth is,
you'd let me.

i fear
that life is tearing us apart at the seams
and love won't be enough
to keep us together.

because i'm pulling in one direction
and you the other, and it's starting to seem like
we're not cut from the same cloth after all.

and although we've been trying
to patch things up for a while—
sewing the holes that keep on appearing,
holding on to the few loose threads of love
still connecting us—

i fear
it's only a matter of time
until we unravel.

the night feels icy without you,
but the truth is, you were my sun.

AND NOW YOU'RE GONE.

is there anything but darkness ahead?
is there anything but coldness left?

i've lost count of how many mornings
i've woken up to a midnight sky
and spent the entire day searching for stars.

because it's been so dark since you left
and i keep wondering if the light
will ever come back on.

it's true when they say
you don't know what you've got till it's gone,
because i never expected there would be a day
when you weren't by my side.

but change found us before i was ready
to let go of things the way they were,
although there's never a right time
for heartbreak to happen.

one minute, we were falling in love,
and the next, we were falling apart.

one minute, it was us against the world.
but now, it is the world against us.

and we're fighting a fate
that's already been sealed.

MY HEAD

KEEPS

TELLING ME

YOU'RE WRONG

FOR ME,

SO WHY

DO WE FEEL

SO RIGHT

IN MY

HEART?

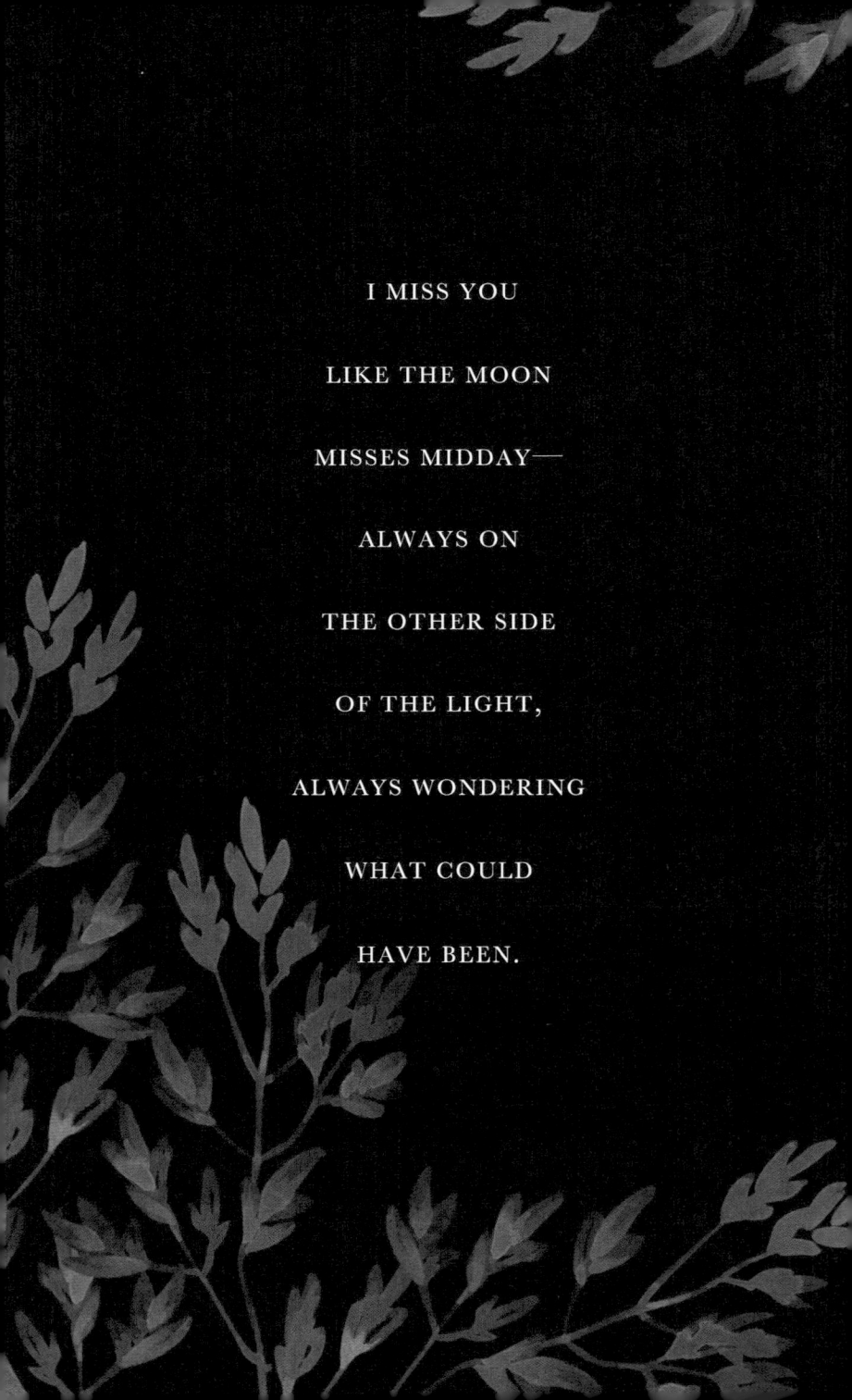

I MISS YOU

LIKE THE MOON

MISSES MIDDAY—

ALWAYS ON

THE OTHER SIDE

OF THE LIGHT,

ALWAYS WONDERING

WHAT COULD

HAVE BEEN.

i keep searching
for a life i can never have
and losing myself along the way.

i fill my head with
the kind of daydreams
that longing turns into nightmares.

i fill my heart with
the kind of hopefulness that disappears
just when you think it's within reach.

but i have never known
how to let go
of a dream.

i have never known
how to find the sun when my thoughts
are so caught up in the clouds.

i grew up believing
that no dream was out of reach,
that my hands could hold
whatever they longed to touch.
my head was always in the clouds,
and my heart was always full of hope.

but growing up
was a falling back to earth,
and in the crash landing,
dreams fell out of my pockets
like coins landing hope side down.

and now, no amount of chasing
the lost seeds of dandelion wishes
or scanning the sky for shooting stars
can bring back the hope i lost along the way.

WHAT

DO

YOU

DREAM

OF?

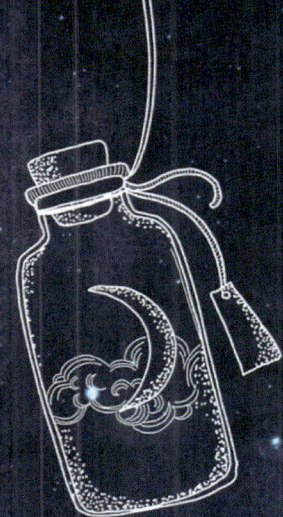

all the ways we never made it

and all the ways we could have.

the days seem to disappear
before i have truly
gotten to know them,
and this is just another evening
that leaves too soon,
taking the sun with it
as it closes another door.

because time is slipping
through my fingers
like the sand of an hourglass,
and it never waits
for me to catch up.

SABINA LAURA

the trouble with me is that
i will keep searching for you
in all the places you'll never be.
i will keep searching for you
even though you don't want to be found.

but you will be in the last place i look,
and my heart won't know how to give up
until it finds you.

WE WERE A STORM

THAT COULDN'T DECIDE

WHERE TO LET THE RAIN FALL.

I NEVER WANTED TO LET GO

AND YOU DIDN'T KNOW HOW TO STOP.

the sky turned grey
when you left,
and for a while,
the rain didn't stop pouring.

time has passed now,
along with the storm,
but i still miss you even when
the sun shines.

WE WERE LIKE

THE BRIGHTEST SUNSET

EVER SEEN

FOLLOWED BY

THE DARKEST,

LONELIEST NIGHT—

BEAUTIFUL

IN SO MANY WAYS

AND DEVASTATING

IN SO MANY OTHERS.

i don't know
how to say *goodbye* to you
when our *hello* didn't get enough of a chance.

i don't know
how to accept losing you
when knowing you is so incredible.

i don't know
how to let go of you
when i'm still so in love with you.

i don't know
how to believe we aren't meant to be
when we're everything i want.

i leave doors open behind me
and the porch light on,
hoping you'll find a reason
to come home.

because you feel within reach when
my heart insists on keeping you close.

but there's a fine line
between dreams and reality
and you are always
on the wrong side of it.

i never seem to know
where i should be going
or which way is north
because every compass
i hold in my hands
only ever points to you.

i'm lost and it seems like
you're not coming to find me.

we are a sun and a moon
in a sky that won't stop trying
to keep us apart.

maybe if we never give up
reaching, the universe will
bring us together.

maybe if we hold on
to all this light we are made of,
one day we will be able to find each other.

— *eclipse*

i'd give anything for us to go back
to the beginning of our love story.

i'd keep almost all of it the same—
the way falling in love *consumed* us,
the way we knew each other by heart,
the way every moment spent with you
felt like a dream come true.

but then i'd cross out the paragraphs
where it began to change.
i'd rip out the pages
where you walked away.
and i'd rewrite the last chapter
so that it *wasn't* the last chapter—

so that our love story
would be immortal.

life

is

filled

with

fleeting

things

and

i

always

want

to

love

them

forever.

FEET

on

i talk to the stars about you
when i miss you too much to sleep,
and they tell me that i won't be
living under these shadows forever.

because with just a little hope
and a lot of strength,
i will discover that all the light i need
is already within me.

you give me glimmers of hope
that i keep holding on to,
but a heart isn't made
to carry this much longing.

there's only so much waiting it can do
before it has to give up.

there's only so much dreaming it can do
before it has to wake up.

i have outgrown so many of the
s p a c e s
i still shrink myself to fit.

but as rain falls
from the lavender clouds
and the earth begins to grow,
i am reminded that letting go
can be beautiful.

after all,
there are some parts
that were never meant to stay.

i'm still wondering
where we went wrong
because our love felt strong enough
to survive anything,
but it seems that the universe
didn't believe we belonged together.

i just hope that one day
i'll look back at this time
and finally understand—
we were just a piece in a puzzle,
a chapter in a book,
a drop in an ocean.

maybe there's a bigger picture
waiting for us both.
and maybe it'll be even more beautiful
than us.

*my heart isn't ready
to stop loving you,
but my head knows
it's time to say goodbye.*

I HAVE

CRIED

WITH THE

RAIN.

NOW

I WILL

GROW

WITH THE

FOREST.

letting you go
feels like losing a part of me,
but then i remember how refreshing
the rain feels when the sky
has been holding on for too long.

so i become the cloud
and you become the downpour,
and i know that soon,
this emptiness will feel
more like weightlessness.

TIME MADE STRANGERS OUT OF US,

BUT THE SUN AND THE MOON

SHINE BRIGHTER APART.

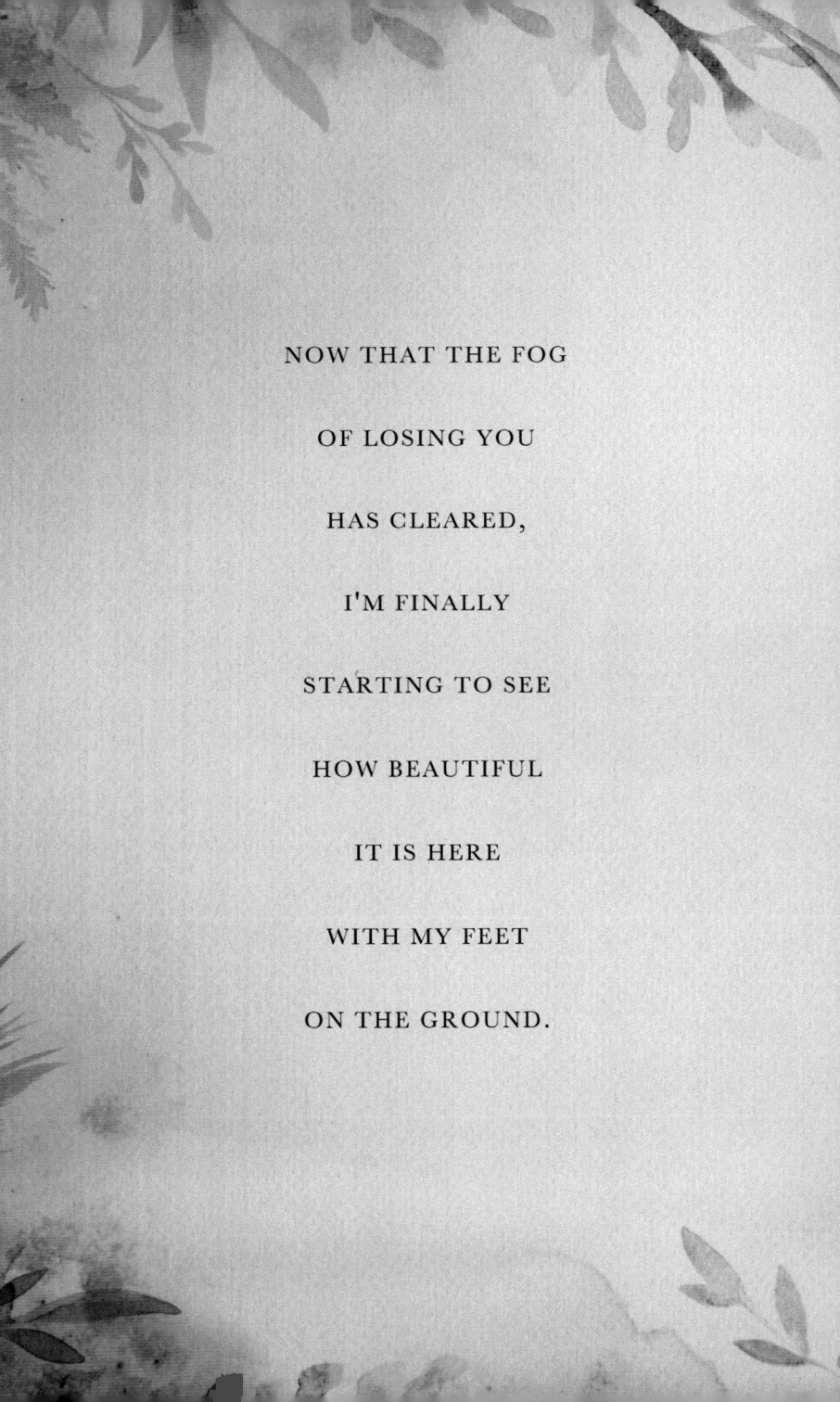

NOW THAT THE FOG

OF LOSING YOU

HAS CLEARED,

I'M FINALLY

STARTING TO SEE

HOW BEAUTIFUL

IT IS HERE

WITH MY FEET

ON THE GROUND.

sometimes i still miss the pieces i left behind, even though deep down i know they don't belong. my heart shattered so i could let them go, but they were a part of me for so long that i can't help but feel a little lost without them.

because *goodbye* is always the hardest word to say, even when you've needed to say it for a while. and it's even harder to hear it back, even when you know it's coming.

but i've realised that letting go takes courage, and it's okay if it hurts at first. after all, leaving parts of yourself behind may cause you to feel empty for a while. but healing will fill those spaces in the most wonderful ways you can imagine.

WHEN HOLDING ON TO THEM

BEGINS TO HURT

AND YOU KEEP FINDING

MORE AND MORE REASONS

TO LET GO, KNOW THAT SOMETIMES,

YOU JUST HAVE TO RUN

AND NEVER LOOK BACK.

i am leaving you
where you belong.
i am leaving you
in yesterday.

because my heart
is full of tomorrows,
and none of them
have room for you.

i let you go
when the weight
of loving you
began to break me.

because some people
aren't meant to stay,
no matter how much you long
to hold on to them.

and although my palms
may feel empty right now,
i know there's a new future out there,
just waiting for me to grab it
with both hands.

*love yourself
enough to know
when letting go
is the kindest thing
you can do
for your heart.*

this heart finally feels free,
like the birds that fly to new homes
with the change of every season.

because learning to let go of you
was an unlocking of the cage door.
an unfurling of these soft wings.
a greeting from the open sky.

and i am no longer searching for you.
i am too busy enjoying the view.

— *on top of the world*

once enough time
and enough healing
had passed, i found myself
able to see the heartbreak
through different eyes.

finally, i could be
happy that we happened
instead of sad that we ended.

and now,
i feel so privileged
that we got to love each other,
even though we didn't get
to keep each other.

LOVING YOU

WILL ALWAYS

BE BEAUTIFUL,

BUT LOSING YOU

NO LONGER HURTS.

MY HEART

HAS BEEN RESTING,

LIKE A SLEEPY

MIDNIGHT SKY,

BUT NOW IT'S

A RISING MOON—

NOW IT'S COMING

BACK TO LIFE.

it takes so much courage
to ignite a new flame after
being badly burnt before.

but your love
makes me feel like
i could walk through fire.

— *the risk worth taking*

*they told me
that the best things
always take time,
and when we crossed paths,
i finally understood.*

*because the dreaming was worth the wait.
the waiting was worth the dream.*

for you, i am
breaking down walls.
opening gates.
unlocking doors.
brushing away cobwebs.
rolling out red carpets.
inviting you in.
hoping you'll stay.

for you, i am ready
to be a home.

WRITTEN

in

the
STARS

i'd been making wishes and wondering
whether any of them would come true,
spending the days searching for rainbows
and the nights for shooting stars.

then we met.
and it was like opening the curtains
on the first spring morning of the year
and letting the warm sun kiss my skin.
it was like hearing a new song
for the first time and instantly knowing
it would become my favourite.
it was like finally coming home
after being lost for so long.

and i knew then
that the universe had been listening.

YOU ARE

the reason i remember how to find

THE SUN

on the cloudiest days.

YOU ARE

the reason i remember how to find

THE MOON

on the darkest nights.

what makes him feel like home?

the way he keeps finding me over and over, no matter how lost i am.

in the end it doesn't matter
how many times you break.

rebuilding will always be
something to celebrate.

you make even
the hardest days feel magical,
because you illuminate a path for me
when i feel lost in the darkness,
and i know for certain that i will
never get tired of following your light.

*you keep loving me through every phase
and i keep loving you through every season.*

*they say all good things must come to an end,
but look at how we've proved them wrong.*

i never knew how glorious
the ground could be until i met you.
because everything here grows and blooms.
everything here feels steady and safe.

i had always lived in the clouds,
never knowing whether i was free
or just lost, but now i realise—
you are the gravity i never knew i needed.

you bring me back to earth
when the clouds call me.
each time, it becomes easier
to keep my feet on the ground.

— *when reality finally feels better than dreams*

i think the universe knew
how much i needed someone like you.
that's why she lit a path of stars
through the night, forming constellations
that connected my heart to yours.

IT WAS ALWAYS MEANT TO BE.
IT WAS WRITTEN IN THE STARS.

every day
brings a different view,
but nothing ever changes
when it comes to us.
because the first thing
my eyes and heart do
when i wake up
is search for you.

whatever the weather,
i know i can face anything
with you by my side.

if you are the shore,
then i am the waves.

i will always come back to you.

everything that once looked
f r a g m e n t e d
through these kaleidoscope eyes
now dances in shades
i never knew existed,

and i realise
that it's less about
what i can see,
and more about
how i choose to look at it.

when i'm feeling lost,
i put my faith in fate.

because i like to believe
there's a reason why
life has put me on this path.

i like to believe
hope is an atlas
and my heart is a compass
that will always lead me
to where i belong.

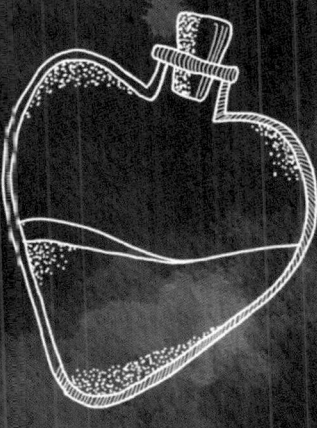

i had always been
too good at hiding, but
you were the first person
who made me feel
worth searching for.
you were the first person
who made me feel found.

— *hide and seek*

don't give up hope
when you've drifted out of orbit
because there's always time
for the stars to realign.

one day, you'll find yourself
in the right place at the right time,
and healing will be close enough
to reach out and touch.

there is something about
y o u & m e
that just feels so right,
but i think the universe
brought us together for a reason.

after all,
how could i not believe in fate
when i get to spend this life
loving you and being loved by you?

every moment is magic.
every second is stardust.

— *i am the luckiest person alive*

I AM

A FOREST

OF HOPE,

AND ALL THE

DEEPEST,

DARKEST

PARTS OF ME

ARE BRIMMING

WITH IT.

*whenever she felt trapped
in the blackness,
she built a new horizon
out of hopes and daydreams.*

*then she ran towards it
with her arms outstretched,
knowing she would
always find a way.*

I FOUND YOU

SOMEWHERE BETWEEN

THE CLOUDS

AND THE STARS.

BECAUSE

ALL THESE DREAMS

LED ME TO YOU,

AND THEN ALL

THE CONSTELLATIONS

ALIGNED.

there is nothing i want more in this life
than to keep spending it with you.

i want to watch the seasons change around us
and grow together in every one of them.

i want to hold your hand through all the years
because nothing could possibly tear us apart.

i want to wake up to you every morning
and fall asleep together under the stars,
knowing we get to do it all again tomorrow.

and i want to spend every day loving you,
because i still have so much love left to give
that even forever wouldn't be long enough.

you are my sun
and all i want to do
is hold your hand
while everything falls
into orbit around us.

let's see where this takes us,
even if we get lost.

as long as we're together,
i am always home.

*and even after all this time,
our love story is still
my favourite dream come true.*

thank you for giving these words a home x

ALSO BY SABINA:

When I Fall

Along The Way

Moonflower

All This Wild Hope

Shades of Sorrow

Silver Linings:
poetry, affirmations, & gentle reminders

A little sunshine and a little rain:
A poetry journal

ABOUT THE AUTHOR:

Sabina Laura is a writer, poet, and illustrator from the UK. She fell in love with writing and language at a young age and went on to study English Language and Linguistics at university. She is the author of eight books. You can find her on social media: @sabinalaurapoetry.

Printed in Great Britain
by Amazon